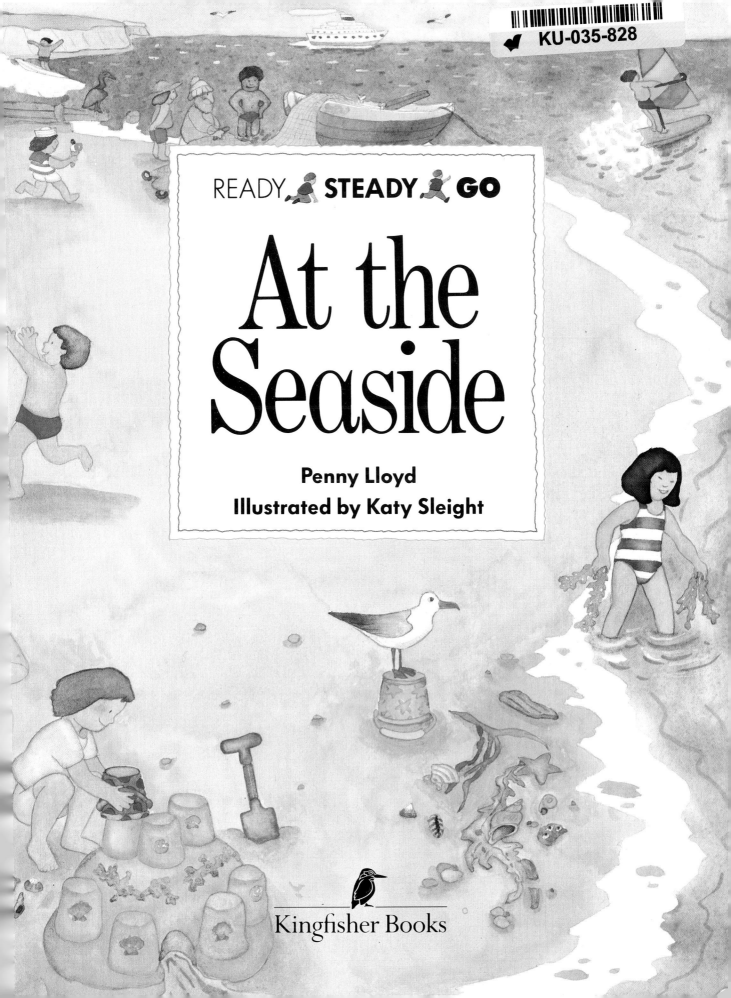

Ready STEADY GO

At the Seaside

Penny Lloyd

Illustrated by Katy Sleight

Kingfisher Books

Contents

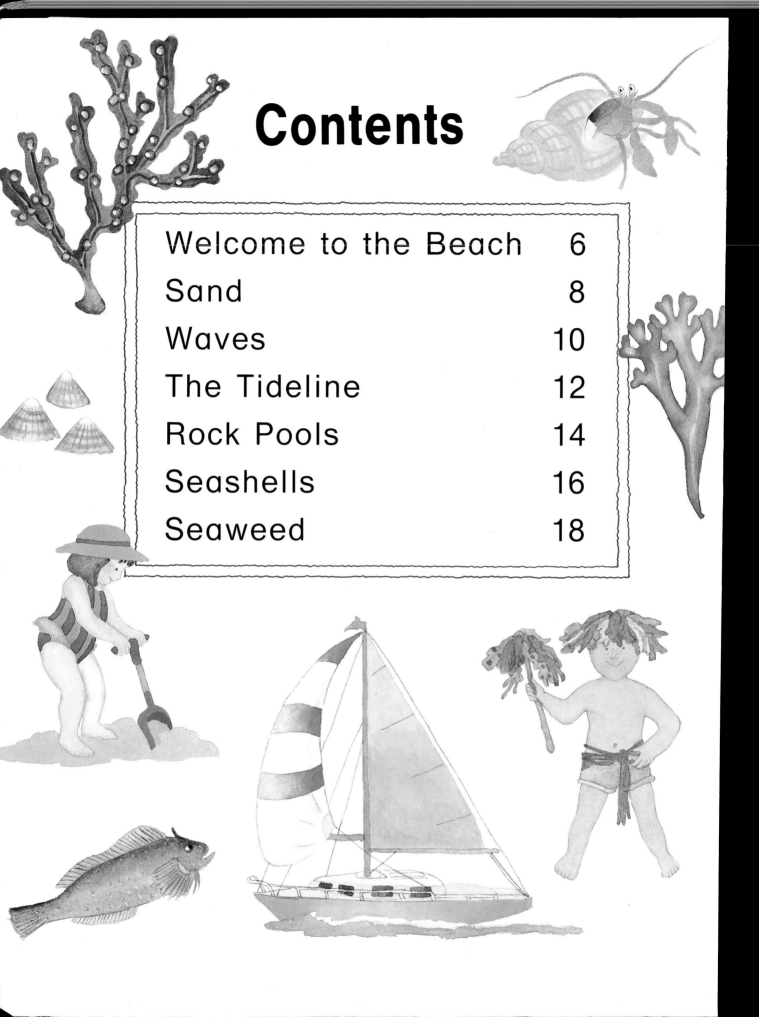

Welcome to the Beach   6

Sand   8

Waves   10

The Tideline   12

Rock Pools   14

Seashells   16

Seaweed   18

At the Seaside

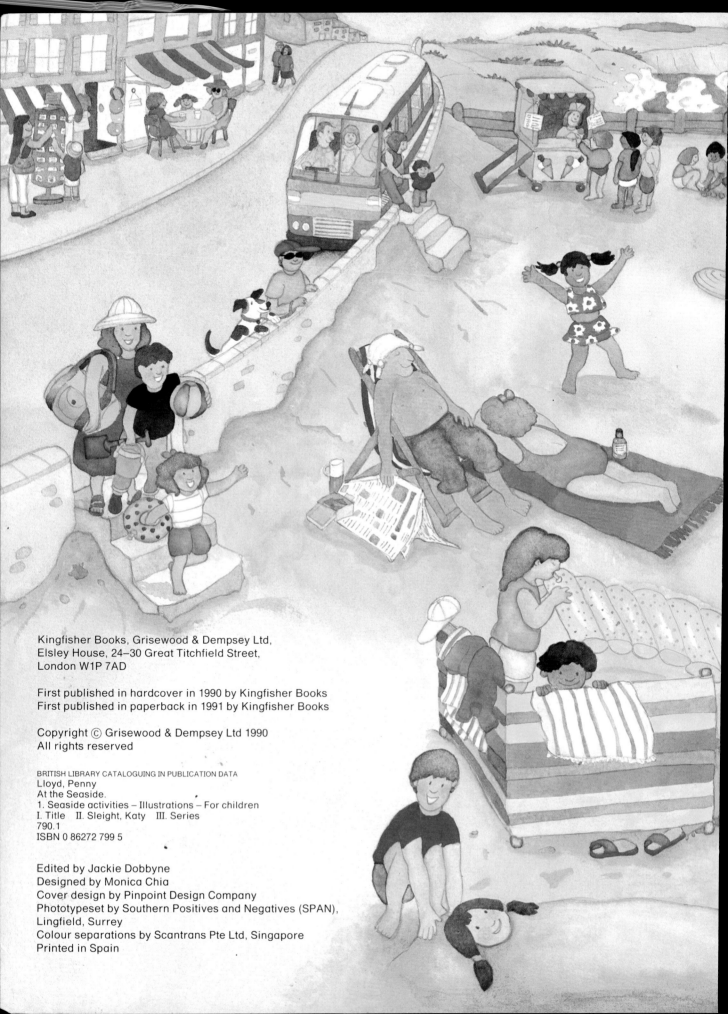

Kingfisher Books, Grisewood & Dempsey Ltd,
Elsley House, 24–30 Great Titchfield Street,
London W1P 7AD

First published in hardcover in 1990 by Kingfisher Books
First published in paperback in 1991 by Kingfisher Books

BRITISH LIBRARY CATALOGUING IN PUBLICATION DATA
Lloyd, Penny
At the Seaside.
1. Seaside activities – Illustrations – For children
I. Title   II. Sleight, Katy   III. Series
790.1
ISBN 0 86272 799 5

Edited by Jackie Dobbyne
Designed by Monica Chia
Cover design by Pinpoint Design Company
Phototypeset by Southern Positives and Negatives (SPAN),
Lingfield, Surrey
Colour separations by Scantrans Pte Ltd, Singapore
Printed in Spain

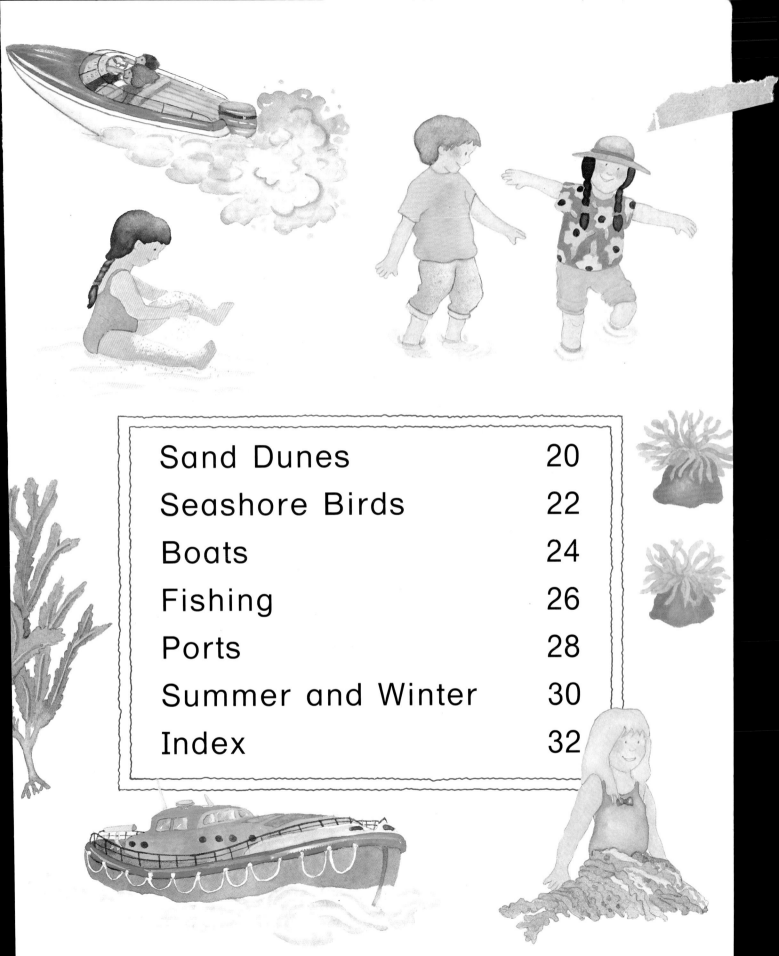

Sand Dunes	20
Seashore Birds	22
Boats	24
Fishing	26
Ports	28
Summer and Winter	30
Index	32

Welcome to the Beach

Can you find these things in the picture?

Sand is soft.

Sand has shells in.

Sand hides worms.

Sand is many
different colours.

Waves

Waves are good to splash in . . .

. . . and to jump over.

They wash away sandcastles . . .

. . . and tickle your toes.

Waves break on many different shores.

Waves can crash . . .

. . . or gently ripple.

They carry animals . . .

. . . and toss boats at sea.

Where have you seen waves?

11

The Tideline

The tide comes in twice a day and the sea covers most of the sand. When the tide goes out again the waves leave treasures behind.

Some of the things left behind by the tide.

Cuttlefish bone

Seaweed

Goose Barnacles

Shells

Driftwood

Can you make a treasure chest?

Bag of shells

Shoebox

Paintbrush

GLUE

Paint

Glue

TREASUR

12

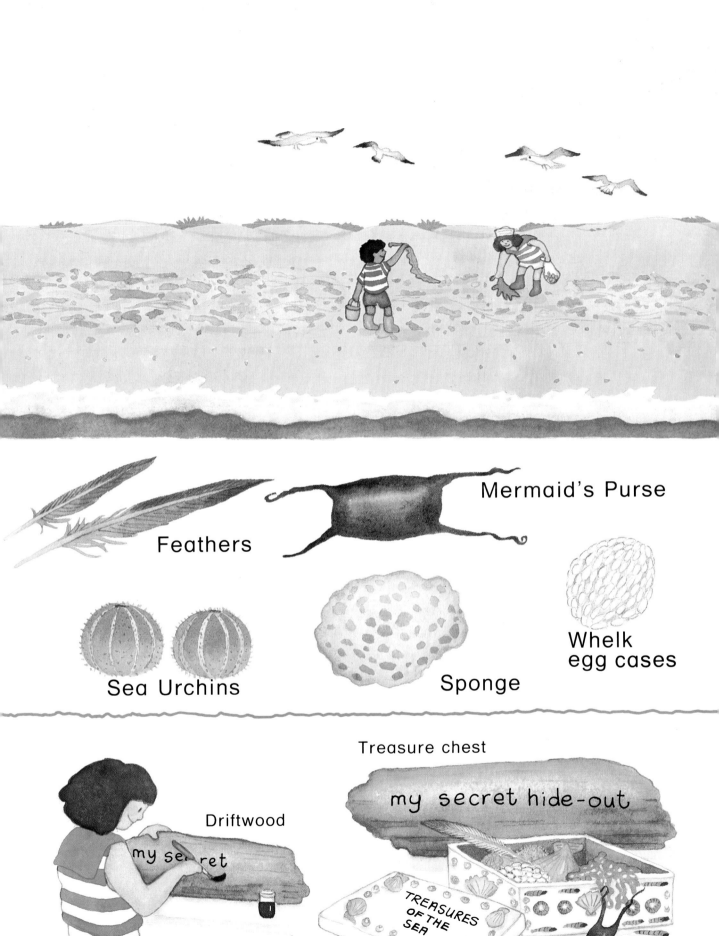

Feathers

Mermaid's Purse

Sea Urchins

Sponge

Whelk
egg cases

Driftwood

my secret

Treasure chest

my secret hide-out

TREASURES
OF THE
SEA

13

Rock Pools

When the tide goes out, the sea leaves pools of water among the rocks.

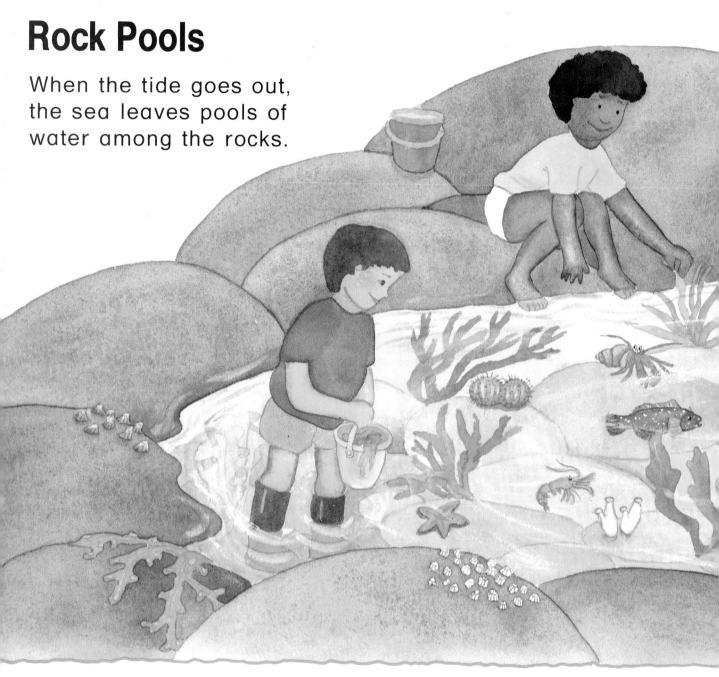

Can you find these animals in the rock pool?

Shrimp

Acorn Barnacles

Sea Squirts

Crab

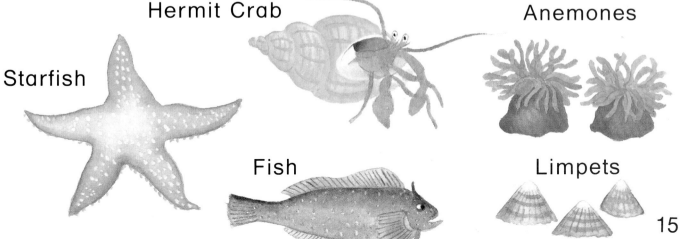

Hermit Crab

Anemones

Starfish

Fish

Limpets

15

Seashells

Many animals which live in the sea have shells.

Sometimes the tide leaves empty shells on the beach.

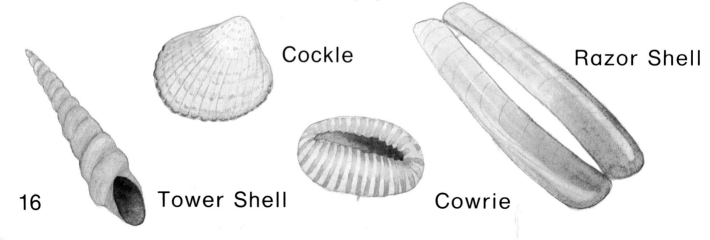

Cockle

Razor Shell

Tower Shell

Cowrie

Can you find these animals in the sea?

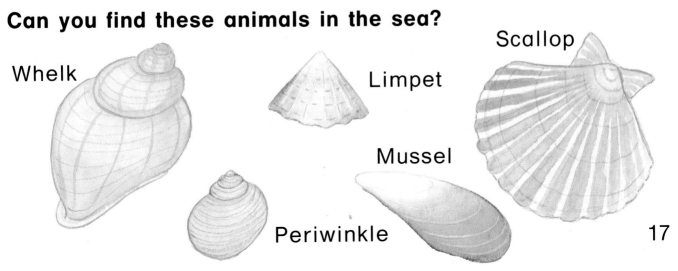

Whelk

Limpet

Scallop

Mussel

Periwinkle

17

Seaweed

Seaweed grows on rocks. Sometimes rough waves wrench it off the rocks and leave it on the beach.

Sea Lettuce

Bladder Wrack

Coral Weed

Sargassum Weed

Kelp

Here are some things you can do with seaweed.

Pretending to be . . .

a mermaid

a pirate

Neptune

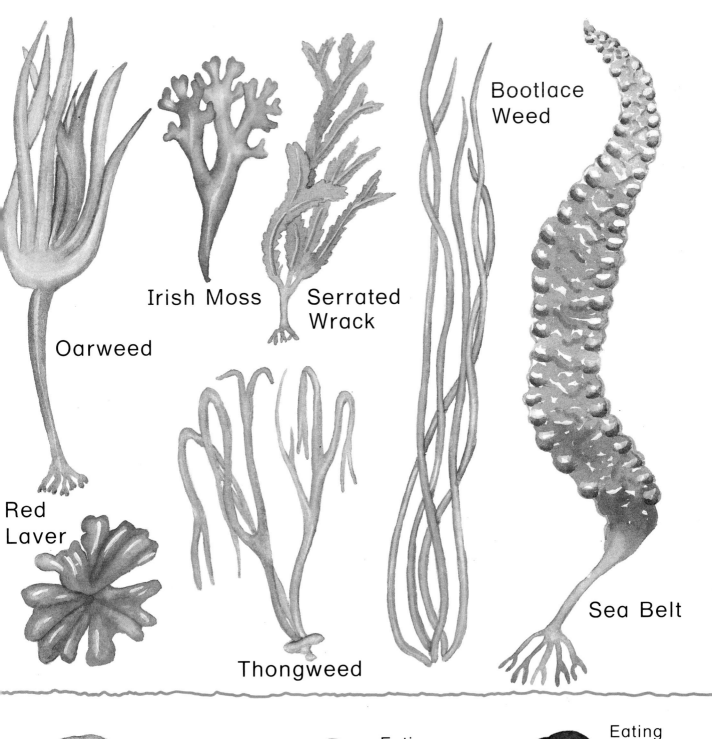

Bootlace Weed

Irish Moss

Serrated Wrack

Oarweed

Red Laver

Thongweed

Sea Belt

Making a picture

Eating laver bread

Eating seaweed with rice balls

19

Sand Dunes

On the edge of some beaches are hills of sand, called sand dunes. Sand dunes are covered in plants which help keep the sand in place. Many animals live on the dunes. How many can you see in this picture?

Can you find these flowers and grasses?

Thrift

Sea Pea

Sand Couch Grass

Sea Sandwort

PROTECTED AREA

DO NOT WALK ON
THE SAND DUNES.
USE THE WALKWAY
PROVIDED.

Sea Holly

Gorse

Sea
Bindweed

Marram
Grass

Seashore Birds

Gannets dive.

Plovers paddle.

Terns swoop.

Oystercatchers wade.

Puffins swim under the water.

Which birds are we pretending to be?

Soaring

Gliding

Diving

Swooping

Seagulls
wheel and soar.

Kestrels hover.

Dunlins
circle and glide.

Cormorants
stretch out
their wings.

Sandpipers
skim the water.

Sanderlings
scurry along the seashore.

Stretching

Scurrying

Paddling

Wading

23

Boats

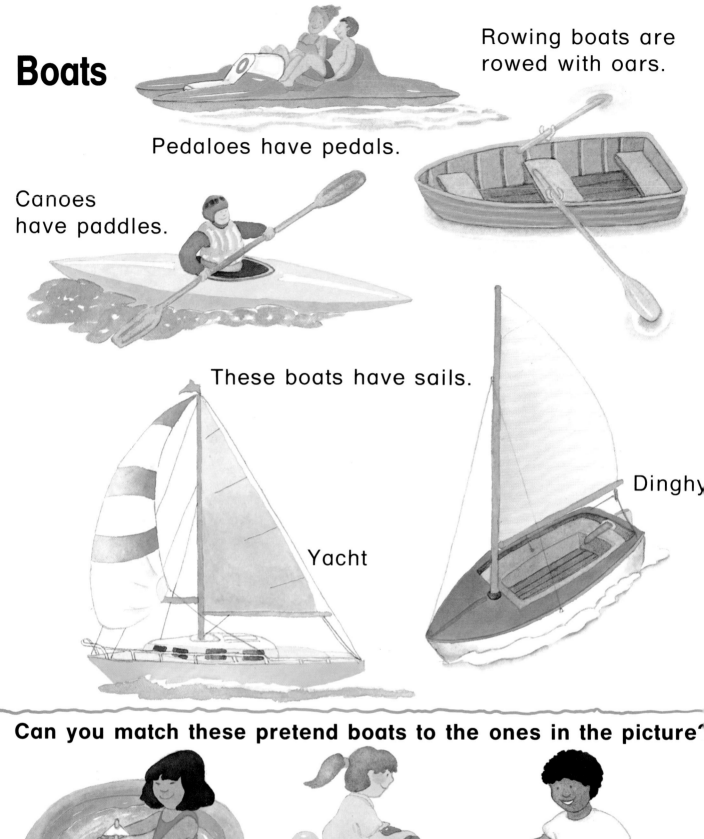

Pedaloes have pedals.

Rowing boats are rowed with oars.

Canoes have paddles.

These boats have sails.

Yacht

Dinghy

Can you match these pretend boats to the ones in the picture?

These boats are powered by engines.

Speedboat

Motor cruiser

Lifeboat

Ocean liner

man overboard!

Fishing

Fishermen bring their trawlers and fishing boats into the harbour at the end of the fishing trip. They unload their catch at the quayside. Some of the fish is bought at once. The rest is packed in ice, loaded on to lorries and taken to the fish markets.

Warehouse

Pallets of fish

Refrigerated lorry

Trolley

Forklift truck

Fishing rods

Lobster pots

Motor boat

Trawler

Fish stall

Mending nets

27

Ports

At the port cargo ships are loaded and unloaded and people board cruise liners, ferries and hovercraft to travel by sea.

Passenger ferry

Foot passengers

Crane

PORT STATION

Cargo ship

Hovercraft

RESTAURANT

Cars

Camper van

29

Summer

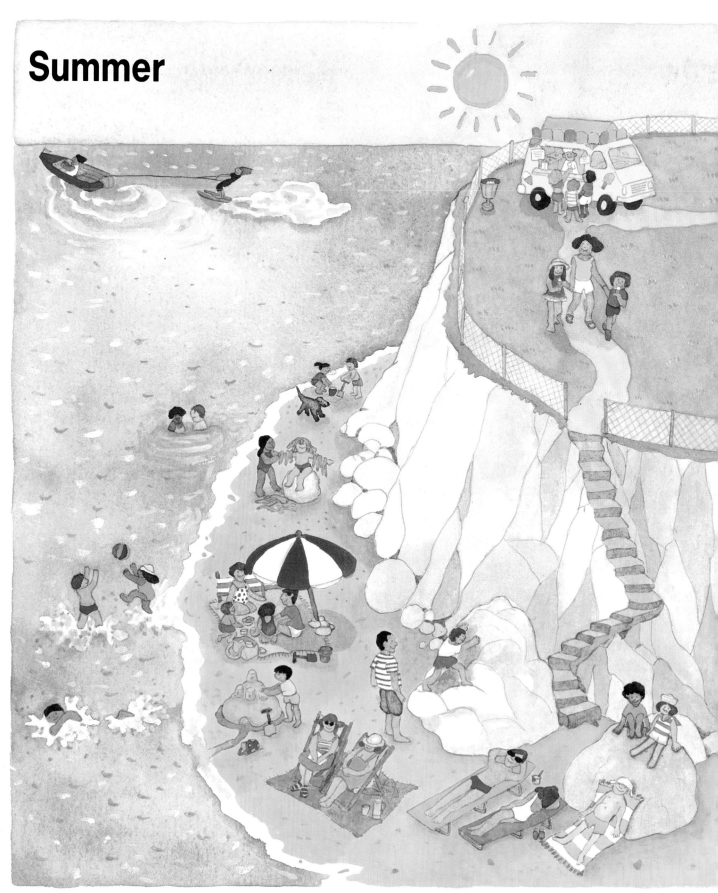

Here is the seaside in summer and in winter.

Winter

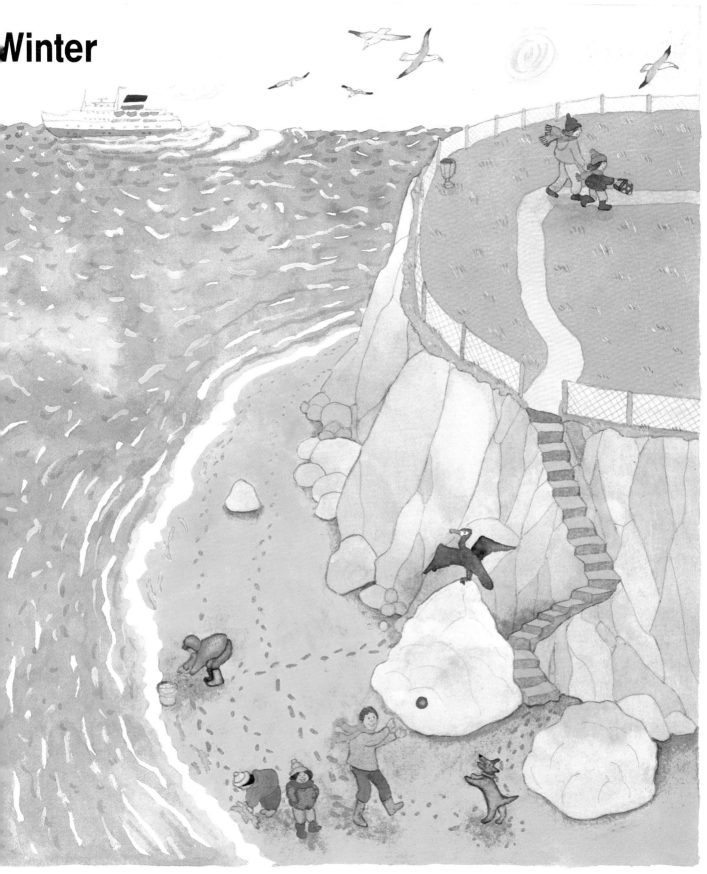

Can you see the changes?

How many fish can you find on the coral reef?

Index

You can find all these seaside plants and animals on the pages listed below.

Acorn Barnacle 14
Anemone 15, 16
Bladder Wrack 18
Bootlace Weed 19
butterfly 20
caterpillar 21
Cinnabar moth 21
Cockle 16
Coral Weed 18
Cormorant 23, 31
Cowrie 16
Crab 14, 17
Curlew 20
cuttlefish bone 12
Dunlin 23
fish 15
Gannet 22
Goose Barnacle 12
Gorse 21
Hermit Crab 15, 16
Irish Moss 19
Kelp 18
Kestrel 23
Limpet 15, 17
Lugworms 9
Marram Grass 21
Mermaid's Purse 13

moth 21
mouse 20
Mussel 17
Oarweed 19
Oystercatcher 21, 22
Periwinkle 17
Plover 22
Puffin 20, 22
rabbit 21
Razor Shell 16
Red Admiral 20
Red Laver 19
Sand Couch Grass 20
Sand Lizard 21
Sanderling 23
Sandpiper 23
Sargassum Weed 18
Scallop 17
Sea Belt 19
Sea Bindweed 21

Sea Holly 20, 21
Sea Lettuce 18
Sea Pea 20, 21
Sea Sandwort 20
Sea Squirts 14
Sea Urchins 13
Seagull 7, 23, 27, 31
seashells 7, 9, 12, 16–17
seaweed 7, 12, 14–15,
    16–17, 18–19
Serrated Wrack 19
Shrimp 14
Sponge 13
Starfish 15
Tern 22
Thongweed 19
Thrift 20, 21
Tower Shell 16
Whelk 17
Whelk egg cases 13

> If you look closely at the picture above you will find an emperor angelfish, a scorpion fish, a butterfly fish, a parrot fish, a lyre tail wrasse, a yellow-tailed blue damsel fish, tomato clown fish, a banded pipefish, a cardinal fish and a surgeon fish.